Smeared Eyeliner & Faded Lipstick

4 embracing growth
Second Edition

Copyright ©2010
Fortitude Publishing

Smeared Eyeliner & Faded Lipstick

Published by
Fortitude Publishing
Washington, DC
www.fortitudepublishing.com

Copyright © 2009 Caneeka E. Miller
Second Edition Copyright © 2010 by Caneeka E. Miller

All rights reserved. No part of this book, contents or cover may be reproduced, or transmitted in any form or by any means, electronic or mechanical, including photocopying, recording, or by any information storage or retrieval system without permission in writing from the publisher.

This book is subject to conditions that it shall not, by way of trade or otherwise, be lent, resold, hired out or circulated without the publisher's prior consent in any form of binding or cover other than that in which it is published and without a similar condition being imposed on the subsequent purchaser.

ISBN: 978-0-557-10968-5 (First edition)
ISBN: 978-0-9830102-3-4 (Second edition)

Cover Design: Elizabeth Irby/*Exclusive Innovations by EI*/
EIbyEI@yahoo.com

Scripture references are taken from New Century Version of the Holy Bible.
Reference Jimmy Cozier She's All I Got © 2001 J Records.
Reference Fathers 4 Justice US website.

Printed in the United States of America.

Prayer gives birth to visions

"The Lord answered me: "Write down the vision; write it clearly on the clay tablets so whoever reads it can run to tell others."
Habakkuk 2:2

Dedication:
For mending broken wrongs and writing the manuscript to the play…

FROM THE AUTHOR

Dear Reader:

I want to thank you so much for purchasing the second edition of Smeared Eyeliner & Faded Lipstick. Every experience in my life has shaped me into the person, the woman that I am today. I hope that something I have written, an experience I have encountered and decided to share with you somehow changes your life. I pray that insight will be granted and that you will embrace your growth in and out of life's call to action. Remember the voice you have been given and use it for a cause greater than yourself!

Thankfully yours,

Caneeka Elleanor

Table of contents:

i. College Rule p. 21
Eargasm
Athleticism
Action
Ink Blot Ink
To be destined
Daydreaming
Inspired
Paper
Union of Isaiah & Justice
White Lady
Something to share
Tender Love
On Accord
Arrogance
Expansion
Tribute: These Shoes
Justice
Mic-Check

ii.   Smeared Eyeliner p. 55
Wonder[ful] Woman
Breaks
Post Relationship

Protection
Headed to work
Naïve
Stream of reality
Visitor
My Biggest Enemy
Free-dumb
Beastiality
212F
Tree of Life

    iii.   Faded Lipstick p. 77
BIG
Damn the Metaphorical bush
Dust Biting
She[lter]
Barefoot & Naked
I am a reflection of him…
Psalm 147:11
Infatuating-Love
Call her ME
Ghostwriter
Identity
Funky Fresh
Surrogates
Let your mouth do the walking
The Battle
Change of Pace
February 13th

iv.   Samiam p. 107
Upper Body Toning
A verse in Feburary
No Spring Cleaning
Deuces Wild
Resurrection
The Big Bang
Movement
Billie
Fate
When I bust a rhyme
For the record
I had stopped breathing
We, me, you
Deadly Silence
Punctuate my High note
Metamorphosis
Aorta

BEHIND THE MAKEUP

I. COLLEGE RULE
Getting higher on education

eargasm

coming with that fire every time it hits the pad.
sexy when i'm good, dirty nasty when i'm bad.
not afraid to do it in places, open to the public.
sitting on the edge, of a leather cushion cusps.
wet, flowing down, to the very bottom of the tip.
working with a fine tool, silent as it drips.
signing my initials, writing my name on every inch.
eyes unable to see the shape, slowly needing to squint...

                                                    4 the art of writing

Athleticism

I have silenced sins so that saints won't seek my soul.
Grew braces over my back to help my bones become better billboards.
Showcasing my beauty that, because of your complaints,
I had to cease from expressing evermore.
I planted voice boxes on the back of my brain so that I could respond to your thoughts that were watered down with bad soil.
Holding onto roots that wither in all seasons of the year.
Rocking steady so that body language will never be confused with miscommunication. Your face speaks volumes while your heart empty, silent, barren.
You have forgotten the importance of better to beloved than bitter, boring, and beating the bottom of the bucket.
The word "Because" stopped being an answer when grandmothers stopped letting children be their best friends and started **switch**ing pops and "painches" up for silent dinners, empty corners, and toys that had words in them...
we call them books.
You have misplaced your values, your respect, and your peace of mind for a millisecond of time

that you think will leave me broken, distraught, lost, and lonely.
But little do you know...
I wear one catcher's mitt...

                        4 catching vs. throwing it back

action

keeping kodak creations stored away for tomorrow.
causing constant confusion as I dwell upon my sorrow.
while we weather through the storm, saturated, and soft.
lackadaisical laughing low, always getting lost....

4 movement

Ink blot Ink

I'm yearning,
burning,
learning how to be.
I'm calling,
as I'm falling,
yet I'm balling my eyes out
as I find myself 8ft. deep.
I'm buried beneath this confusion
and I'm constantly losing
while I'm choosing what's right and wrong.
And it won't be long
before the beat of my song
is thumping against the back of my neck.
And my car crashes against man made walls
and when you realize there's no one to call
you die
and
wreck.
Well
one comes before the other
and according to my mother
procrastination will be my biggest down fall.
So don't be upset
if
I'm not there with you for the long haul.
How did my situation get to be,
like India Arie,
a

complicated
mel
o
dy.
My bass lines and treble clefs are all I have left
as I sing myself to sleep
as I wipe the tears that leak
from my pores
the doors constantly open and shut in my face
But
I continue to chase
my dreams
with intention to grab hold of them
and
ride the blue wind
because
everyone you meet
is not
your
friend
and
I want to bring this to an end
but
I
can't
just
yet
I still have a lot on my chest.
And
there's milk in my breast

as I feed you what you need.
You're the root of all evil
and
they call you
greed.
You bleed from me my poetry
verse after verse
ink
blot
ink
stroke after stroke
giving you rhymes to make you think
And
someone should drop me a line
because
the merry-go-round goes round
in the opposite direction
riding backwards
on the ground
You watch me pass you by
and yet
that's all you seem to do.
I'm learning about this girl
but even I
can't
tell
you
WHO...

                                                4 the right stroke

To be destined...

Sometimes I'm so deep
I drown in my sleep
with lyrics invading my brain
as I ride the poetic subway.
That takes me by my surprise
as I constantly wear my disguise
you people look me dead in the eyes
breathing slowly
losing life.
You think you know but you don't.
You want to ask me but you won't.
I let you down slowly but surely
immediate loss of hope.
You crawl before you walk.
Steady cursing but can't talk.
Dead just as sure as you live.
Outlined in white chalk...

4 the future

daydreaming

and even though i looked both ways before riding
out into the oncoming <u>traffic</u>
            i still missed the lanes.
and even though i put my <u>car</u> in park to prevent
from hitting that train
            i still ended up on the tracks.
and even though i can ride my bike, no training
wheels, no little tikes
            i still ended up on my back.
looking through one brown eye at the world
higher than myself
the metamorphosis of clouds,
a cotton puff moving to the left.
the wind blowing everything
except this body of mine.
Horns telling me to Go
Wasting time at the GreenLight...

                                      4 Waking up

like Sunday morning…

Inspired by your spirit
sent to me from HIM
infected without ointment
mending wounds I can not heal
Finding myself afraid that I'm into this too deep
nostalgic,
as if we've met before,
in a former life,
on similar streets
confused of my understanding
how you and I
we're two peas in a pod
two leaves on a branch
though sounding it is odd
underestimating our bond
the love we Honestly share
Spiritually connected,
with souls,
that are clothed
naked.
and.
bare.
with eyes full of water
from the Rivers we have crossed
mouths dry
full of Sand
from the Words that we have lost
pockets

digging
deep
from the price that this costs
Minds growing by the Second
from the Lessons that we have taught
Peace be within you
all the joy you have earned
Laughing like lovers
from the poetry we yearn.

                                                     4 r.e.s.t.

Paper

Because ink bleeds through me like you do when
your lips touch mine
&;
i'm trying to make you a permanent factor in my
life
like
this tattoo i've created of words just for you.
i have no idea why i'm turning my body into a
notepad
probably
because the only way i'm looking is down.
my heart frowns because it misses
your touch,
your feel,
your passion,
your sex appeal
this s*** is real.
and what is real to you might not be my reality
but
i can't stop thinking about you writing your poetry
on me.
Ruling me,
blue lines run from one side of my body to the
next as you make circles on my breast.
i've checked out my options and no one else
compares to you.

laying flat on your bed,
use me,
wide ruled....

                                                    4 creativity

the union of Isaiah and Justice

YOU don't matter to me
because
tonight,
tomorrow,
and
so
on
I'VE got the VICTORY!
HE is powerful enough
to
have
saved
me.
YOU might not comprehend
because
YOU lack the ability.
YOU people try to tear me down
with your trampled ways.
BUT
little do YOU know
that
todayhasbecomeyesterdayand
YOU
cancloseyourearsbutyouwillstillfeelwhatihavetosa
y
BECAUSE
infectious
this spirit WILL find YOU.

Buried underneath your daydreaming
as
GOD
continues to tell
YOU
TO
s t o p w o r r y i n g....
BUT
YOU
don't
listen
BECAUSE
YOU
don't recognize
HIS
voice.
Excuse me…
Pardon me…
but
I'm married to Isaiah
and
he's given me no other choice
than
to inform YOU.
BECAUSE
the moment is NOW!
"Preserve justice, and do what is right"
BUT
clearly you don't know how.
"My salvation is about to come, he says,

My righteousness is about to be revealed."
"Blessed is the one who does these things,"
I thank YOU for the full course meal.
YOU continuously motivate me
despite what set backs YOU'VE brought:
"My thoughts are not your thoughts,
and
my ways are not your ways.
Just as the heavens are higher than the earth, so my
ways are higher than your ways,
and
my thoughts are higher than your thoughts"
(Isaiah 55:8&9).

                                                      4 peace

White Lady

I live for the lines,
white, blue, red, use green, whatever I can find
simply me, simply divine.
You miss out on the experience, you miss one for the times
She wants you for her gratification but I need you for mine
Wasting quarters on bad head game but you can't resist me because I'm a dime.
Focusing on your balance at the base of my spine.
Whoever said love is blind wasn't opening their eyes.
Snorting your existence, pumping your love into my arm.
People don't understand; they misjudge your charm.
I say you bring me joy, they say you put me in harm.

But what do they know anyway…

They've never felt your straight and narrow
Never been lost behind your bars
They don't know the feeling, that lines can make stars.
I live for you; will die for the ink
F*** those that hate and all that they think.

Lines take me places only minds expanding could understand…

> 4 hallucinating

Something to share…

I write rhymes to rhythms with heartbeats that resemble my own.
A history so rich; a deep red, like the dirt on roads my ancestors' tears turned into clay.
A state where laws are backwards.
Progression behind.
Values conservative,
Nonetheless,
We call it home.
Learning that our beginning is how we were able to achieve our now,
Voices growing louder as we express what we have to say.
> Collaboration, our connector
> Family reuniting, our friendship
> Different places, our creativity
> Each other, our inspiration

We write rhythms & blues in the hearts and minds of our children's children.
We etch words of love and unity into their souls so that THESE moments will not be taken for granted.
We believe in one another so that one another can continue to believe in the dream deferred.
We encourage growth, strength, spirituality, and power into each person who has our name flowing through their veins.

And we stand proud, unashamed, and confident that our legacy will be one that will continue to be passed on for generations to come...

4 identification

Tender love

I have lived this life,
trying to save three different worlds.
Two little boys,
and
one little girl.
No one can hear them,
their cries people ignore.
Focusing on the surface but I'm trying to reach the core.
It amazes me,
the rotation,
how we beat around the bush.
We want to save the children but keep our feelings hushed.
I brushed the hair from their eyes,
to help them envision their future.
Questioned them about life,
asking to see if they're sure.
No one ever asks how they feel,
their opinion about their life.
People ignore them and assume their cries don't equal strife.
I look at them and see me,
often misunderstood.

Misplaces, misused, a princess living in the hood.
My ghetto is someone else's castle or the other way around.

Took me a lifetime + life times for the joy that I
have found.
No one thinks to talk to the children
because of fear that they won't listen.
Passing them by as their eyes fill and glisten.
It's hidden for you to seek,
but the game you often lose.
Two boys and a girl; you put yourself in their
shoes...

4 Reaching One

On Accord

We use them.
We discover them.
Riding across pink trails.
Flying off of salmon cushions.
We kill souls, that never had a chance to survive, with them.
We encourage winners towards losers from beginning to end.
We need a manual of direction on how to appreciate their existence.
We would probably lose it because we are careless individuals.
Selfish in our own right because we can't give credit where credit is due.
We're users.
We're irresponsible.
Until we can learn self control…
We will always be a slave to words and never come to a Common Ground.

4 Living

Arrogance

No matter how many men I f***,
Really don't press your luck it's not that easy.
No matter how many cats want to squeeze me,
Drop on their knees to get in between these,
Thighs,
Jaws dropped, tongue out, and eyes wide.
Breathing hard from the excitement inside.
Most men claim they won't because of too much pride.
Until they meet me, then themselves they surprise.
Orgasm landing on the tip every time.
Swallowing slowly in a hip-hop rhyme.
Beat boxing of hearts because the rod never lies.
The grin of the Grinch because many may try.
I tell them goodbye.
Because.
No matter how many men I mentally f*** with,
No one will lay it down like you…

4 real stimulation

Expansion

She flows freely like friends watered down.
Wanting a little more, than some cheap coke and crown.
Wanting, just like you, some sleep that's a silent sound.
But only missing you, as you firmly stand your ground.
Spelling out let's try, without you saying why.
Giving you the most, without filling you up with lies.
Jokes that have no punch lines, chorus' with no hooks.
Beats with no rhythm, a library with no books.
And anyway she wants to look,
Rolls eyes that her momma shook.
Robbing men , a crooked crook.
Burning water, a lazy cook.
Riding bikes but forgot to duck.
Running a marathon while running amuck.
Losing money, low on luck.
Killing toy soldiers, a Tonka truck
Give me some green and call it a buck.
Lost in the forest, a gingerbread hut.
Throwing you a phrase and you label it pluck.
Breeding our minds…
And they call us all muts…

                                      4 opening our minds

These Shoes...

It's about taking a stand.
Just as clear as we are able to stand each day.
It's about dreaming bigger than what's possible.
Making a way out of no way.
It's about where we might be headed
when we leave from these stomping grounds.
It's about what your legacy will be,
when you no longer will be around.
It's about appreciating our blessings
without the trailblazers,
where would we be?
Stop and think about HER strength;
A spirit that's set free.
STOP and realize that tomorrow isn't promised,
express your thanks here and now.
Remembering a woman so courageous,
Vivian Jones,
take your bow.
Everyday walking the University,
whatever minority you represent.
Everyday think of our liberty,
her freedom,
and what it meant.
Everyday that we have life,
is a day to celebrate.
Let's be the authors of our own stories
Chapter 1: To Graduate.
Let's remember what it took

sweat will ALWAYS get you change.
May your soul rest in peace
here's to you,
Amazing Grace.

                                            4 School house doors

Justice

i KILL them with this weapon.
it's SHARP and ill with wit.
THEY claim to be ready for me,
but they can't take this shit.
i STAB them with my lyrics,
and
CUT them with each line.
confused before they know it,
FLOORED,
DEAF
and
BLIND.
SHOOTING out these BULLETS,
a blue or black ink.
making them CRY with every stroke,
FEEBLE when i wink.
SPRUNG off my swagger,
MESMERIZED by my walk.
RUNNING over emotions,
with every sound of my talk.
i keep them in constant FEAR
because
they WONDER what my next move will be.
but they just can't figure it out;
it's just the
E.S.S.E.N.C.E.
of me...

4 the feeble

Mic-CHECK

sassy Sisters secretly share Sentiments of Solitude.
speaking words that surround peace for
S.E.R.E.N.I.T.Y.
Reflecting on the E.S.S.E.N.C.E. that we exude,
each step,
on this lifetime journey that awaits our arrival.
One person **Eight** their pride & swallowed it
whole;
digesting on the humility it takes, any way the
wind blows.
One person **Eight** inequality & stood for all
mankind.
The world is larger than *just us* women & someone
needs to take the time;
to liberate the wronged & celebrate JUSTICE,
for all who wallow with whine.
A complicated workload keeps everyone afraid,
that tomorrow will backtrack their prints,
But we follow behind the ELITE,
ELEVEN women, who God sent
to,
Pioneer a chapter, which many have grown to
love.
The legacy of Lambda Zeta, none other can rise
above
the,
changes that we've made, the wrongs that we've
right,

the darkness that we shared before we reached the light.
The relationships we build, lasting beyond our grandest thoughts.
Soldiers in this battle, which someone else has fought.
Sharing enough to learn,
that you and I alike
discovered through Delta Sigma Theta
the ability to keep things tight.

4 anniversary lines

II. SMEARED EYELINER
Tears don't let the water roll off of their backs like ducts...

Wonder[ful] Woman

walk.
this way.
when words wrap around my wheels,
on the brain cells that produce wisdom.
We fight wars for **weapons** that the **mass**es can't understand.
while Wives and Children die before they were suppose to be called.
Women wear veils to hide the bags they wear on wounded hearts.
whatever makes you smile whenever we're in separation.
We lie dying our hair different colors to hide our natural age.
without peace making strategies,
in order to save the world from withering into isolation.
And we **Wonder** what **Woman** didn't stop to complain...

            4 being appreciative

Breaks

There's a man I know, whose heart is on the rocks.
A soul deeper than the Pacific, without canal locks.
A mind of pure intelligence, infatuated not.
Loving deeply me, trapped, held down, caught.
He doesn't understand his beauty, he's blinded by his ail.
He holds a heart of stone, security he can't inhale.
Outside you'd never know, inside he emotionally aches.
That's the deception of appearance, these are the breaks.

4 being stone cold

Post Relationship

i only want what's best for you but you always
push me away.
i'm tired of walking that path with you
trying to think of what to say.
and when the words make their way
you always shoot them down to death.
taking my inhaler
as i'm running out of breath.
and you'd never understand
because
you hear what you wish.
you're thinking love is lovely
but
deep inside i'm pissed.
i'm tired of being tired of this
the bull,
the arguments
and
such.
sometimes this gets hard for me
you know
dealing with the breakup.
you always want to talk
and see things from your view.
talking without listening
as you're looking for a clue.
and no i never guide you
because it's not that deep for real.

the aftermath of you and i
this is how i feel.
sometimes i get scared
because
they said i couldn't do it again.
i've prepared myself for the loss
without even thinking i could win.
i find myself,
not me,
being someone else's type.
trying to live for the two of us
confused about this life.
and i couldn't be your wife
because
there's so much more to that.
trying to move forward
as my heart still looks back.
tired of trying to coach myself into letting you love
me more.
closing every window
just to crawl out the door.
loving you too much to even love to let you go.
the more we continue this merry-go-round;
the friendship continues to grow.
and it's impossible to be friends
with someone who has your heart.
mending all the pieces but it still falls apart.
wanting not to call you
as i press the one touch dial.
needing to be arrested

as i'm sitting through this trial.
moving on slowly
meeting someone else.
haven't done this in years
actually needing help.
but i'm not allowing myself the chance
to know him on any level.
still trying to put you in place as i'm saying,
"us again, never."

                                              4 keeping promises

Protection

Have you ever just wanted to curl up and
die,
curl up and
die,
curl up the ends of your hair and
fly
into tomorrow
where the beginning is bitter sweet.
Where the sun is warm enough to cool your inner
needs.
Just curl up your eyelashes and
dye
them a tar baby black.
Curl up in the corner and
die
to never come back.
Just curl up and
cry
and uncurl
but
cry
some more.
Die
because of fear of the
unknown
yet
to be explored...
like

my now,
my tomorrow,
my yesterdays,
my life.
Just curl up and
die
before I
attempt
to try...

                                                    4 beauty salon's

Headed to work

I bathe in Jacuzzi tubs alone,
I shed tears within the walls of my closet,
I have mastered crying in silence and pulling
myself together,
I light candles only to blow them out;
No love making until the flame burns out,
no,
just sitting until the next time I light them myself.
I find comfort in holding myself, sometimes at
least.
I find pleasure in rubbing my own back.
I live for this moment but at times I wish I
would've chosen another one.
But I press.
I get dressed.
And they call me.
Wifey...

4 new personalities

Naive

Suffering from a black eye, bruises on my arm. Marks around my neck, sometimes love can bring you harm.
But I love him and he loves me, how do I know, he told me.
Scratches on my face, swollen from head to toe, I can't feel my body a love that no one knows.
There's a lump in the back of my head and I have a few broken bones. True love for some comes different, for me it comes in blows.
But I love him and he loves me, how do I know, he told me.
I'm jumping in my car to leave, but I always keep going back.
The love that we had was strong, but the pain I endured was black.
But it's better to be loved, than to not have anyone at all.
I love him, he loves me, I know because he slams me into walls.

(save me)

4 ending violence through education…

Stream of Reality

This is dedicated to:

All the bulls*** that you fed me,
you bled me,
me ahead of me,
withheld me,
I kept me,
wept for me,
slept with me,
lied to me,
I cried for me,
inside I died for me,
lost pride with envy,
she left you breathless,
I gave you my air
and
you still didn't f****** care!
I wear my emotions
without going through the motions
have me dry with lotion
as I'm drowning in this sea of quicksand.
You melt me,
only I can help me,
I felt me,
slipping into the point of no return
and you f****** let me,
you left me,
I'm running in the opposite direction

trying not to fall
as I crawl to you.
I'm calling you,
you pick up
and hang up
without knowing that I knew.
She's mentally f****** with you.
She's f****** you and you let her,
but I'm clever
and I've peeped the s*** too.
I'm tired of these liars
as I'm hooked up to plastic wires
with no magnetic force
on this pre determined crash race course.
Yelling at decibels
I can't even fathom
as I'm losing my voice
where the f**** are my choices,
hopeless
I'm needy,
eating this s*** up as if it will complete me.
I'm starving,
this pain,
I'm pissed the f*** off
and it's beating my brain.
And it's raining,
left out to dry as I'm literally hanging
on the edge of this cliff,
and I THANK YOU for giving me the lift,
I'm flying with this gift

and I won't be denying your lies
and I'm tired......
of this.....
so f*** you.......
you're fired!

                                        4 the best he ever had

Visitor

Victimizer in this game of lies.
Honesty, not a reality of my own world.
In an atmosphere too unhealthy to live, in a home unmade a house...
My victims are you, yourself, mind and soul.
I come at you in dark, while your mind is idle, body relaxed.
I tell you how precious you are and you believe me.
I lead you into dark caves, mysterious like midnights eyes.
Hidden behind a crimson veil.
  I.
    am.
      your.
        insecurities...

                4 the boogey (whoa)MAN

Blame Shifting

I promised myself
and
I swore to HIM
that I wouldn't mention your name.
And through all of the fortune and fame I blame myself.
It's my fault you haven't called
because
I'm living behind this wall
that I will never let fall
and
I blame myself.
For loving you more than me.
Explicitly.
Loss integrity.
Woke up one morning and I thought I was free,
from your pain and stress
and I thought I was blessed
but it's my fault.
How I allowed myself to get caught up in these wires,
loving a liar,
who always inspires
that painful side of me,
that poetry
of eternally
being
at

peace.
And I blame myself...

4 pointing in the wrong direction

Land of the Free

> "my country tis of thee
> Sweet land of liberty
> To thee I sing…"

They named her Stephanie* Marie,
Because they believed one day she would grow up to be,
The number one defense attorney,
In this disabled country,
We call America.
Stripes of red and white streaming down her leg.
Blue beats her heart, so she might as well be dead.
Addictions she can't shake,
with legs glued together because she's terrified to be raped…
Again.
Hair covering her face,
so that she and the background can just blend.
And never be treated, like a true American citizen…

4 Optimism

Bestiality

giving me the inspiration,
to release my frustrations,
of this manifestation
that
just
won't
stop.
and I won't let you beasts get the best of me,
making me feel like I'm lost underneath.
and if you want to know the truth,
stop believing your lies,
getting high off this sh**,
and that's just it...
wanting you to do more with your life,
than attempt to be someone's wife,
that only wants you when it's cool,
standing butt naked in his room.
and honestly your union was doomed when you broke up,
then came back again.
and again you tried again.
yet again you couldn't win.
but you can be the fuel,
that sets me on fire.
I'll be the tool you claim me to be,
you can continue being in denial
                                    4 not moving on

212° F

you give me the fuel to light my fire
you liar
these wires
are connected
to
my
heart.
you probably don't believe
that when I was conceived
God created me to have
one
of these.
But through all of the deception and deceit
I can see how you **could**n't **be**
all I wanted **you** to **be**.
And I know this isn't the army
but
I was hoping that you wouldn't battle
But surrender.
Instead you've been a hindrance
to my soul.
And
this
fire
continues
to
grow.

                                          4 turning up the heat

Tree of Life

Trees in the winter look like an elephant's grave yard,
in which the King Lying, has barked away enough leaves,
only to stay.
And I yell out the wrong plays in order to get to the right place.
I spray you with mace so your reaction won't be late.
I wipe away the tears from my ears because
until you stop beating my drums,
I will never be able to hear.
Your face creates a line of sweat across your hairline because
They're not even sticking with your sap…

4 value

III. FADED LIPSTICK
Love: Energizing my exhaustion

BIG

At the end of the day.
When the lights dim.
Words fade.
and
the smokes clears my airways.
He chooses her.

But...
my food was good enough for you
when cookbooks couldn't teach her well enough
to feed your aching belly.
Peanut Butter and Jelly was more than just a song
but all of the things she brought wrong to the
table.
Unstable in your decisions when my kitchen was
the one you cleaned
and apparently
things always go the way they seem because
my heart kept telling me to set you free but
your Damn Ass wouldn't leave.
You wouldn't just let me be,
instead you were building me up to believe,
that there was a potential for you and me.
You wanted to live the dream.
Your intentions might not have been,
to leave me dry and empty without a pot to piss
in,
but you did.

But
I was too busy trying to see the man inside of a kid...

                                      4 wishing on the Zoltar

Damn the metaphorical bush...

I can't do this anymore,
love you from afar.
Yes,
I
said,
love...
No need to continue lying to myself,
can't deny what it was.
I mean
what it is
and this affair has me failing my own quiz.
Giving myself tests to make sure I match up,
to the standards I've created,
a passion so corrupt.
And hell yeah this sucks,
because I don't like the control you have over me,
you have no idea,
that you make my knees weak.
And my stomach does back flips, somersaults, and cartwheels.
All of this in me,
a reality that's so unreal,
and it's clear to me,
that,
you and I could never be.
I looked in my glass,
deep into eternity,
and there I saw you not standing with me.

Or me standing there without you by my side.
Your purpose for being here has me outside of my mind.
And God knows I've tried and tried and lied to her that is me and cried and died and came back to life,
a woman incomplete.
Lost without your compassion but don't worry,
I will find my way.
Confessing this to you,
of course,
moments too late.
I hate every part of me,
that loves and yearns for you.
I hate I'm still writing,
I hate you have no clue.
I hate you for being,
the prototype of what I want.
What I need,
what I feel
moments undone.
Poetry un-flowing,
Rhymes without a beat,
paper with yellow lines,
pens with no ink.
But a writer writes on,
like the lyrics to my life's song.
Even when I'm write,
my punctuation is still wrong.
Even when I love you,

from far inside my soul.
Undressing the artist,
artwork put on hold.
I can't have you now,
it's just not meant to be.
Too good to be true from day one I knew.
I knew,
I flew,
I blew back towards the wind,
to push this lost heart,
back to where it could mend.
Except the pieces missing,
are the ones I don't need.
I'm wiping my eyes from the desire I bleed.
The visions I've seen from the blind mans eyes,
I hate you for this for my internal cries.
I wear a disguise but it's falling to parts.
Eating up the food in my grocery store cart.
And I push that pain inside and make sure I don't throw up.
Nausea and fever have me sh** out of luck.
As I still continue to write and it pisses me off because this time I can't stop.
The words flow down, before it makes sense to not.
It drops like the blood from my nose.
Putting tissue in all of my holes, making sure everything stays closed.
But I can't get to my heart and it's just as open as the sky.

Letting you love you,
hell,
let me stop trying to imply.
These implications and this damn metaphorical bush.
I'm sick of hiding behind and keeping my mouth on the hush.
You've made me blush and I'm quickly turning pink.
Through my caramel skin I can't hardly breathe or blink.
I'm cleaning out my closet but wanting to hold onto this.
You are the light of my life,
my joy and my bliss.
I kiss you as you sleep because I want to be in your dreams.
Dancing along sienna colored sand, writing with red ink.

4 gardening

Dust biting

Potentially you are all i NEED YOU to be.
Nice hair, sized feet, even [accomplished your biggest dream].
But how can i wife you, your baggage weighs US down.
Potentially WE could, but in reality, WE'D drown.

Potentially your qualities are easy enough to change.
WE have the basics: Physical Attraction
And that's enough to maintain,
OUR,
potential relationship i'm potentially hoping works out.
WE should probably drop the haters; they say faith can't work in a crowd of doubt.

Potentially you could love ME, I mean, there's no need to rush.
You've know MY love for *3* years yet *you've. kept. yours. on. hush.*
i LOVE your modesty, it can potentially make ME blush.
As long as there's a possibility, WE can bang until we bust.

So.

I'LL keep going with this charade because now I'M in it too deep.
I'VE already planned OUR future while behind my back you creep.
Insecurities tell me to sit tight because I'VE already wasted so much time.
Forgetting how the script goes so I let YOU feed me the lines.
The ones that say, "come see you" when I know I should walk away.
But the POTENTIAL seems so PROMISING that, I instead, decide to stay…

                                        4 run on conclusions

She[lter]

You love what you shouldn't because when your heart tells you where it should be you laugh in the face of honesty.
Fear will only get you so far in a shell that you've let me penetrate only to regurgitate my existence in your life.
She's.
Safe.
For.
you.
But.
I'm.
The.
Truth.
I'm the one you chose to lean on when
wind storms caught you walking and
cell phone companies left you less talking
but more communication with my soul.
We found ways to ride the sound waves,
master the maze,
and complete the courses that didn't allow excuses.
Or even understand what they were.
I'm your new beginning and she's your, NOW.
Your, "next please!!! BUT not right at this moment" because you're scared to step into the world that welcomes all that you are.
All we have grown to be.

All that I am.
Sometimes condoms break leaving you pregnant with a life you only wanted for your right now.
When you play it safe, your heart ends up late.
Soul completely delayed.
Mouth cotton based.
Us no more dazed.
In love a foreign place.
Lost without a trace.
You should've could've stayed.
Let's stop playing these games...
YOU step out.
From playing it safe...

                4 being risky

Barefoot & Naked

I am as incomplete as tomorrow without sunlight
and tonight without the moon or the stars.
And
no matter how far you are,
all roads lead back to…..
I am as incomplete as the last line of the beginning
of this poetry.
And no matter how faint my ink may be.
All roads lead back to….
I am like a run on sentence nothing can complete
me or stop my flow.
NocommaorperiodstillincompleteIwillgo because
All roads lead back to….
You took away your love without consulting with
me.
You could've called me a b****; to drop dead into
eternity.
But the words roll on
no matter how incompletetheymaybe.
Yet and still,
all roads lead back to….
You had me loving you like I've never loved
myself,
like I've never in my life,
loved anyone else.
Running away, afraid of what this could be.
I dot my i so that I won't be incomplete.
BUT that's just how things goes;

"oh the places my heart has seen."
I am like the girl I once knew,
when all roads led back to….
me

                                          4 what it feels like

                    I am a reflection of him

Here like whenever, changing like the weather
Phone lines disconnected, calling me occurs never
Maybe because I'm clever, you need me to make you better
Moving to different stages, using lack there of as your lever
Knitting black and blue sweaters, burning bridges with blazing letters
heloves me especially when herlove doesn't let him
Days get dull, when you find my name
Remember that your sperm is what created such a frame
Embark back on the sex, that moment of conception
Holding me towards the sky such a bitter sweet reflection
wavering between today and extra days that make tomorrow
waves underneath my skin to wash away my sorrow
"Sometimes I love him, sometimes I love him not
I thought I could let you go but you're all I got…"

                              4 avoiding mirrors

Psalm 147:11

I woke up today and decided to let go,
of all the stress and the mess I wanted to know
but decided to guess.
The idea came to me something new, something fresh.
By the order of HIM I know I'm being blessed.
I opened my eyes and I finally saw the light,
peace within me, of all that is right.
Through the evil of confusion, questions I have,
going forward, without looking back.
I prayed for a sign, HE made it clear as day.
Created a path without asking for a way.
Answering my prayers as I fell to my knees.
Opening my heart, as he gives me what I need.
I woke up today and claimed it as new.
No more gray clouds of moments untrue.
I found myself wearing two left shoes.
Walking like God as I do what I do.
But the footprints I leave are ones not of me.
I asked God last night to set my spirit free.
In this service being all I can be.
I woke up this morning with ability to see...

4 trust

Infatuating-love

secretly I say a prayer of in.love.with.you.
So,
Will **you** be mine?
Could you be mine?
Wine glasses sit empty as I stare at the bottles we could **have** but can't.
Because you're in deep infatuation with her...
She finds time for other matters in life while you take notes on my ability to be a wife.
You know you want **me**.
On an eternity time span.
Bands play our theme song while everyone around us sees the right in what you see as wrong.
Because you're in deep infatuation with her...
And she seems like a sweet chick **but** it makes me physically sick that **you won't** leave her.
You won't **take the time** to follow the royal brick road that leads you to crimson rivers.
Never stopping its flow.
Never planning **to say no** if you **just** love me too, a little longer.
My heart can't stop playing deep high notes **for** what could potentially be **us** when you continue to wear head phones...

4 not listening to your heart

Call her: me

Endurance.
Seeking patience from God.
For I know that He has a reason for my existence; my being here.
Learning to love you, using better words from a distance.
Changing at least one person's life, discouraging them from fear.
Instilling the fundamentals, that we deserve respect.
As human beings, women, young and old, slowly we begin to forget.
They say it takes a village, but what if it's already burned down.
We are merely bodies with no substance,
giving cheap dances,
to achieve our objectified crown.

She just discovered her worth, fourteen, and no one let her know.
Your body is not who you are; paybacks aren't worth the pain.
Pointing the finger, for someone else to blame.
She thought that her beauty, carried her further than her brain.
And her friends, formerly known as, are now calling her a low down dirty shame.

Forgetting that her mother, at birth, had given her
a name.
The spirit of God tells us, we are what we claim.
Trying to erase the images, on her skin, it left a
stain.
Digging into her membrane,
believing that most hoes should be called dames,
and labeling herself as such.
Because someone forgot to tell her,
her worth she burns of coal,
is just a diamond in the rough…

                                                        4 identity theft

Ghost Writer

Writing poetry about you on the walls of my shower.
It was that kiss that had us whispering in midday conversations.
Having revelations about us spending our lives together.
Changing like the <u>weather</u>.
Saying something like whatever, every time you claim you <u>love</u> me.
Opening my mouth to swallow this poetry in the form of your tongue
and
it ain't over until it's done
so
let me wash you.
Cleanse you with this bar of Dove,
flying 8th grade love <u>notes</u> over your head
as I make intimacy with you
standing deep in the middle of my bed.
The drain catches each emotion that it rinses from your chest.
Stand still for me
and
let my tears enjoy this quest….
on the walls of my shower.

4 being a ghost writer

  identity

Why is it so hard for you to love me?
I have loved you since before life was given to me.
Before I knew your name
C-E-D-R-I-C
I loved you after your false promises
fake I love you's
and "I will call you backs"
2 years and 9 months later,
I'm waiting,
I love me more
for the father I lack.

                                                    4 emptiness

Funky Fresh

Just when you thought it was safe to walk outside.
Able to ride all of the rides, undisguised, and in
reply to the letter you un-wrote
unlike the written verse
of the curse
you rehearsed
it's worse this time around.
Because every time I pick up my pen
words meant for you
flow out on end
and I can never find the beginning
where this madness all began.
I would, if you asked, without hesitation give you
my hand.
But man,
I mean damn,
none of this make sense.
It's probably not supposed to, I can't even take a
hint.
I can't even pick up the phone and tell you what I
can't say.
I mean I can, I get nervous, I don't know what you
will think.
I speak to you in rhyme because my free verse is
too much.
It bombards you where I want it to, directly I reach
out and touch.

Your beautiful eyes as you see the world I see.
Knowing the potential of the union of you and me.

It scares the living *blank* out of me as I know it does you B.

You have me break dancing and pop locking, spitting rhymes over a dead mic.

You're the beat that gives me assurance, have me dancing all night.
And I will continue to write until my words I can share with you.
Until then B-Boy, keep doing what you do...

4 be-boys

The surrogates (a poem)

I named her "Maxine because she looks just like you."
Wearing hair longer than yours,
with curls to add some flair.
A mole on her face,
in your exact same place,
as if God came down and put it there.
She's a ball full of bubbles, more spunk, more fun,
with the same love you share for him.
And I don't care, which one he picks, because
neither of his chances look dim.
You both love what you don't understand,
wasting time on someone who has a choice.
You seal off your life, ignoring other men, not
speaking because he took away your voice.
So caught up, in a fairytale,
that Disney himself couldn't pen.
Waiting for him at the finish line, but you haven't
yet begun to win.
He speaks,
words of affirmation,
to keep you close to home.
But little do you know,
he's not hurting at all,
because he's found himself your clone.

4 Having a type

Let your mouth do the walking

Closing eyelids to read the words
you have written on my eyelashes.
eyeliner blacker than the coal
in the fireplace you left bare.
Where do you want me to wear these tattered clothes
that cotton left for care.
Share me with him,
let us in, enter into the place
that you would not let the lights dim.
Because your light no longer lights my world
you no longer shine in my direction.
Sex isn't what it could be,
005 should be your section.
Your mouth does a lot
but not enough to make me come.
Walking the way I came loving like we're done.
How is it that you move so nice
when you have yards leading your way
but I minimize the grass that you have to cut
to help you to nicely play?
But every party has a pooper
and apparently it's you.
I could've done it better
instead of hearing you say, "it's cool."

4 getting the big head

The Battle

I can't stop thinking about you,
trying to occupy my time.

Trying to do other things,
walking straight on an uneven line.

Trying to avoid seeing you out,
but wanting to see you so bad.

Trying not to sound excited when you call,
and when you don't;
getting mad.

Trying to keep my heart a float,
not beating outside my chest.

Trying to keep it closed away,
putting my emotions laying rest.

Trying not to think of if you care,
or even miss seeing my face.
Putting my finger on the issue,
but always losing my place.

Trying to read your every move
and the ones when you stand still.
Moving my eyes to avoid your gaze
slowly lacking the will.

Trying not to try to do,
the things I say I won't.
Doing what I want to do,
even if I don't.
Escaping to that part of me,
that never felt this way before.
Getting lost on the journey,
opening the wrong door.
Hiding behind the wall in me,
invisible to the naked eye.

Trying to remain honest with myself
but always living this lie...

4 double lives

Change of Pace

We wait until the moment is gone to begin to love
the beginning of our story.
We fail to write sentences that make sense,
because we are extraordinarily, unusually lost.
We write slowly in a baby's comprehension.
We breathe heavily on an English composition.
We love lightly because we're our only
competition,
Until we end up alone…

                        4 waiting until you're ready

February 13th

if only telephones worked.
when pulse and tone meant two different things.
long distance should be free.
plane tickets should be complimentary.
trains and automobiles should be provided on an extreme need basis.
if the north star really guided you to me.
when constellations actually created outlines of items in the sky.
because the moon only exists in the corner of our minds.
when you thought I was your daughter enough for you to stop bullshitting me with lies.
because you once saw your face in mine. claim my hair as something you gave. if only phone lines moved beyond county borders and state lines then maybe you would hear my cry, you, my funny valentine

                                        4 the disconnection

IV. SAMIAM
Oh the places we'll go...

Upper Body Toning

Like those boys that run in the dark,
I'm trying to reach levels of innocence that
fluorescent bulbs can't illuminate.
Undetected by its glow.
I'm ghostly with my stride,
aluminum with my pride,
right-side-leaning when I ride,
I'm your brain open wide.
Hear my cries when you sigh,
my laughter when you try to lie.
Feel my compassion when you attempt to discover
who I really am.
Give a damn to tell me that you do.
Make the money and I'll share it with you.
Dance on concrete without the shoes.
Act real shy and I'll make all the moves.
Whisper gifts that I dare not to lose
Because WE have built this empire of love...

4 staying in shape

A verse in Feb-ru-ary

I whis-per HIGH COO's
in your ear on spring Sun-day
af-ter-noons. Be-cause
your love goes deep-er than just
five, se-ven, five lines.

                                        4 ear-ly mor-ning show-ers

No Spring-cleaning

We write words while working on loving one another.
More than movies we make in the middle of hearts.
Heating hell's fire so much it gets cooler than,
U and EYE behind lenses on Saturday.
When we'd always choose each other
over cleaning cabinets and cars.

4 Satur-days

Joker, Joker, Deuce

Is that rage on your face, as I cut you with this spade.
Wasn't just talking noise, I am the Jack of all trades.
I include you into my poetry page.
"You know what I mean," I have rhymes for days.
Mind letting go, no more holding back ink.
You lose once again, bleeding pretty girl pink.
This time I won but perhaps next time you might.
Freezing to my toes, in this ice cold fight.
Fire melting water, I will dilute what I made.
Here are 7 books to remember from whence you came.
God brought us to it, Friday, Saturday, and Sun-ny days.
Every time you speak, mind stops in amaze.
A maze leads us out, never met someone like you.
My thought are not your thoughts, but the facts still remain true.
I will make it, do what it do.
Don't renege or again you might lose.
Cautiously make your move.
Better not be sorry, always play it safe.
Words flowing streams, rivers meet as we lay.
Queen to be, my heart, I give to you, crowned King.
Building pyramids in Egypt, flying on the phoenix, we spread our wings.

Like Maya Angelou's bird I break free from this metaphorical cage.
My winning streak finds you, helping you to release your rage.

I'm scared. Putting Shirley Temple curls all over my head.
To hide, to hide, to cover up, to hide, to blend, to mend, not pretend, try to win what I've won.
What's done is done but what's yet to come, to be free is no longer dumb.
Reality sets in, to blend, to win, we WON, a different type of man.
My heart beats, dances, break, no longer, dances on card board boxes, trying not to Run DM-C me in a different light.
I won't lie, I will try to bring you happiness.
I'm different from the rest because I'm JUST
the right one, at the right time, wanting to go the right way with you.
The poetry flows free when the lights are set and dim.
Ask me where I'm going and I will tell you where I've been.
Movement, moving going, to say more, that we are in this together.
I find my meaning, in the words you love to hear rambled.
On the mantel piece, a picture of them.

More than a crush like Kim, deeper than wanting to just be friends…
I don't put periods at the end of my sentences because I like to run on into paragraphs that smiles when they hear you laugh.
I plot specific points on the graph.
Like Spike Lee, she hate me.
On this paper I write rhymes to thee.
Why be "dom" when your mind can be free.
Standing on your knees in a pool that's 8ft deep.
I rock you like Mike.
Check 1,2,3, on the mic.
Love you, I think I might.
Hold me in the middle of the night.
Light of the world guide my path.
Holding your hand, let's make this moment last.
First let me calculate and do the math.
I've cleaned out my closet and taken out the trash.
You make my heart skip and my stomach does flips.
Let's take it slow before I show you the swivel in my hips.
Off my shoulder, you want this chip.
Socially we do, the whirr and click.
You were probably confused but I'm "every woman" kind of chick.
Together we are so ill making everyone feel sick.
Clowns they do tricks but baby we lead the crowd.
Hold up your fist, I'm black loving you and proud.

Putting out the smoke from the cherry black and mild.
I simply ask you why, and baby you tell me how.
You mean this much to Stykes.
Merging poems, up all night.
Losing myself as we keep our love tight.
Growing as one to meet eye to eye.
When I inhale your spirit, I feel this HIGH.
So I will try to keep you happy always.
Carpe Diem baby.
Let us seize the day!

4 Metaphors

Resurrection

in the third month
of the thirty first day
of the third day of the week
in the third year.
i didn't see you.
And you
didn't
acknowledge
me
either…
So
i wear smeared eyeliner and faded lipstick as a
reminder that it's been longer than thirty seconds
plus thirty that we've come to a common place
that didn't drag us down dirt roads where neither
of our hearts should belong.
i write the scarlet letter C across my chest to
remember the moment when we cared enough to
not let enough be the beginning to our end.
When almond aromas from the coffee pot faded to
blend into an item we never used.
When my day and yours create the double dosage
of completion in the form of numerical genius that
neither of us could recognize because, we were too
busy being caught up in the devils screenplay
starring u and
i almost let him win the Oscar until my eyeliner
faded away; and

i almost kissed us to peace(s) but my lipstick decided to stay; and
i almost kicked rocks with your name on it, to stones who gave a damn, when makeup held together more than flaws;
when we remembered samiam...

                                        4 turning water to wine

The Big Bang

we barely write whispers yet we wine about words.
hell freezes in one instant while we summarize what we heard.
you wish you understood but underneath you untie bows
prefer to be called lady but steadily you act like hoes
men can tell the difference between a Mary and the other
we try to call it how we see it yet instead we end up mothers
nursing negative newborns next to naked breasts
nipples never empty as we increase our flattening chests.
discouraged by our differences, ever changing in our growth
trying to see the woman you knew without criticizing God's work
evolving like the earth, excited even to have life
with your reflection, a love that's worth the fast.

                         4 the beginning of change

Movement

Without hesitation I give you a vivid explanation of how facing my life with you is something I wouldn't escape.
Wearing shoes you couldn't chase me in, hoping over buildings so your heart I can win.
Unlike any other the epitome of a good man.
Gogo dancing to the beats of the band.
Let's get married, I will give you my hand.
I penciled you into my master plan.
The little engine that will, I know I can.
Blessed in the pure, so like is just grand.
You think you know but you can never understand.
Sharing a garden on our ancestors land.
Doing hand stands because I love you upside down.
Talking people to death about this man I have found.
Heart ready to beat, when you're ready, we can go.
Mind telling song, let's just take it slow.
Ordinary ways, ordinary us.
Ordinarily I wouldn't say this but I know you I can trust.
Teaching each other, we learn, on the yellow school bus.
Revolution not beginning until we let go of our crutch.

God told me to be patient for HE had something great for me.
Asking God is it you, and if not then who could it be.
Feeling like you are more than a blessing but poetry in motion.
Writing the script to our fairy tale, keeping the lines open…
So let's go!

4 jet setting

Billie

Can we go back to the way we once were?
When words didn't get lost
between our mouths and the receiver,
between our teeth and our lips,
beneath our skin dying to burst through our heart.
I want to regain
the passion,
the lust,
the suspicion;
If we were on opposites sides of the world would
you swim across
Pacific's, Atlantics, Red, and Baltic oceans and seas
to tell me you love me more than this journey we
are taking, together?
Because I can only never stop thinking about you.
Wishing you would kiss me and hold me;
tell me that distance will make us stronger.
Yet will the heart grow fonder?
Or will our minds just wander into other people
and places that God didn't create?
Because having to pretend like our love surpasses
vocal chords we seldom use is getting older.
While this lady is singing the blues...

4 answers

Fate

I should tell you that you light my candle,
standing in my mind,
i can handle,
passing the time.
holding your beats as it pumps,
left
to
right.
As I lose my breath,
become speechless,
unable to catch up,
stomach dances to the flight of the bumble bee
as your spirit reaches me.
The Son, Father, and Holy G.
Renew your mind like ancient remedies.
A man of your word belief that HE paid it all.
Prepared for what's to come,
waiting for the call.
A man I'd never meet
had it not been that he was sent.
Real to the core
while the rest
uncomfortable and pretend.
I bend backwards to stretch my muscles,
crunching to understand.
What do I do now because I think I might like this
man.
Haven't crushed since first grade.
Like this I can't remember.

Wanting to confess
but not wanting to hinder,
This,
friendship we've built,
Not sure where he stands.
Rejoicing for his accomplishments.
Being his number one fan.
Feeling quite weird
for liking someone so much.
More than a sexual attraction,
deeper than any touch.
Sharing this with myself
and God I have to mention.
I believe in infinite possibilities and divine intervention.

                                                4 the possibility

When I bust a rhyme...

You woo me like Jill.
Holding Jack's hand while we conquer these hills.
I want to be sedated, so where is my pill.
Is $.07 enough for a full course meal?
I spend 18 seconds kissing your emotions.
It's too late to close the door so I leave the window open.
I welcome you, I'm hoping, that what feels right is correct.
Giving you my all, sharing with you my best.
You are my peace of rest.
My ear upon your chest.
Whenever you are afraid, baby, you can lay upon my breasts.
I think I say our names on the ancient walls of Egypt.
I had a dream about us in a real life that was flipped.
We are royalty, sitting on thrones, the best tag team.
While others have dirt to dish, we keep it squeaky clean.
Yes, I'm born with it, no it's not Maybelline.
It's because I'm worth it, I love my liberty.
Liberate me and love me like no one is paying attention.
They can't afford to, dimes they keep on pinching.

Clinching to my sheets because I want your arms around my waist.
Let me gaze into your eyes and caress every inch of your face.
I get in play, I'm ready for you, ready to spend forever.
Like E. Badu, you are my orange moon,
baby because I'm clever...

4 Neo-souls

For the record...
I take journeys to lands with no names
and population of "just us"
down the center of your back.
Mountains smooth and warm, like our love;
early mornings, as the sun finds its place in the
sky.
Finalizing its existence
and in that instance your lips cool me,
comforting all hesitation.
I make landmarks on the small of your back to
remind you how passionate I am about my city.
My hometown where I can sit on any porch and
recognize all who have,
been,
going,
coming, to you.
In a matter of seconds I have loved you so much
you love me back as if we have known each other
our whole life
so
swiftly we move forward because when the time is
right people will always think it's wrong
but
we move on.
We love strong because who knows the exact time
frame of how love is suppose to be
or
how soon is too soon, when really it's up to you
and me.

And hell we both agree that forever doesn't make sense without each other so
let's blow our cover and get married.
When everyone else lets you down you can rest your body on my back.
And travel down roads others will never find the map for.
And while they are concerned about how soon we came about,
we will be dwelling in our happiness and laughing at all those who had doubts.
See baby, they don't know that God is our head.
And we consulted with HIM first before laying in this bed.
> *(and if your mind is in the gutter, then you'll never make it ahead. To see what we did and the pieces that we mend)*

See when you don't believe in possibilities so great.
You might miss out on your blessings in a blocker debate.
If that works for you, then you live as you please but my heart knows its place,
I've been down on my knees.
HE confirmed this union and the past is erased.
We write never ending stories while you remain in your place.
So move swiftly…

4 always taking notes

Breathe

Words find their place wherever my pen lands,
no game plan,
hands cup my ears so I can hear what you're saying.
We're playing,
dandy at laying,
steady praying that you and he are one.
Because I'm done with the games,
repeating my name,
cats thinking they can tame
the reality that exists in me.
The rhymes I must release,
I wear you out so call me a beast,
put thoughts in your mouth so why not suck on these.
I had stopped breathing.

*Circulating the "air" my lungs have reason to **expand.***

My heart danced to its own beat.

*Two stepping in the name of love, on national blast, American **bandstand.***

I closed my eyes, seeing the darkness in all prior.

*Widely closed as I examine you to your **core.***

I was a prisoner; being my own guard
and out of no where you appeared.

*And life flows freely through the walls of my **door.***

4 expansion

We, me, you

WE lie in bed naked but WE never touch. WE combourhairoften but WE rarelybrush.
I asked YOU to hold me then YOU turn to dust.
I say,
"let's get married"
YOU say,
"what's the rush."
whenever YOU kiss ME I can't help but to blush. I give it to YOU constantly
without doing too much.
the party just started so I call your bluff that YOU'D rather be here with ME...
Eyes say a lot of words YOU think YOU don't speakmouth making contact to MY lips while WE sleep.
I tell YOU, "go hard"
and you fall in too deep
YOU say, "it's not for the quiet"
yet I told you I was too meek
Sex dripping drops orbits chewing gum gets stuck
YOU wanted to make love but quite frankly I'D like to fuck
Pigs run wild while WE sit like asses because somewhere we lost conversation...

4 quality time

Deadly Silence

I thought I felt your arms around me.
In the midst of the argument; you being pissed, me being me, you held me.
And my tears dried up, my mind stopped racing, my feet stopped pacing the air of love I had been floating on and I relaxed.
For the first time all night I felt at ease.
 I didn't have to try to find the words or find a cool way to say please.
You just did it.
Penetrating your spirit into my soul and heaven only knows how long this will last.
This peace of happiness in being quiet that isn't aggravating like usual.
I inhale the moment to store it in my lungs to have it circulate throughout my entire body.
Sending euphoric oxygen to my brain because this is how we are suppose to be.
So I close my eyes, I fall asleep, only to wake up, and realize it was only a dream…

4 Illusions

Punctuate my high note

Can I be the period behind your S.
The end to all of your sentences.
The transition into your paragraphs.
The comma to make sure you pause.
A rebel without a cause.
Take me,
my beauty,
and all of my flaws.
Dropping panties, you drop the drawers.
Late night talks, long distance calls.

You are the 𝄢 in my 𝄞 .

4 a beautiful song

Metamorphosis

Breasts creating new cups to fill.
Preventing my feelings towards them to grow any larger than their current existence.
From a distance I see uterus expanding, seed demanding a larger place to establish its residence and it evident who runs this operation…
Silencing all sensation I once felt under tender buttons,
between soft lips,
beyond the mountains he dared to climb,
between widening hips;
I'm nauseous.
Watching the person I once understood,
Live, let go, and give into womanhood; We're good.
When she dances on tabletops because inside she feels she should.
Body ever changing as she embraces what God said HE would…

                                          4 finding my libido

Aorta

Our baby has a heartbeat.

A rhythmic melody playing inside of my womb.
Making music to my heart, creating techno,
grooving tunes.
Our baby has a heartbeat that pumps life through
its soul.
Finding strength daily to continue to move and
grow.
Our baby, God sent to us.
Heart beating His Holy muse.
Learning proverbs from my Father,
SELAH,
crimson hues.
Dancing on the water,
cruising through the flood,
discovering its existence,
exemplifying God's love.

Our baby heart beats…

4 entering motherhood

Thank You:

To God for mercy, grace, love, peace, comfort, chastisement, and being THE Father.
To my husband for pushing me into my potential, for loving me unconditionally, for being my #1 fan even when I didn't see what you saw, for being the God fearing prototype of what a husband should be; may our lives continue to run smooth like butter. I love you more than any poem unwritten about you!

To my Aunt LeeLee for having books and random poems in the attic, To my mother for making me read and telling me "Don't put off tomorrow what you can do today" thus encouraging my procrastination, *smile*, to my family, friends, Sorors, and everyone else who has been there, watched me grow, watched me fall, and watched me bounce back because HE has already given me the strength and vision to accomplish the things the devil wouldn't let me see…

I thank you all:
For your words of encouragement, your prayers, your belief, your unbelief, your support, and your love. This paragraph doesn't do JUSTICE to how much my heart wants to thank you.

A special thank you to Yorri Berry and Fortitude Publishing for seeing something in me to bring me on board for this revolution of opening minds and making an impact on the world through the gifts God has blessed us with! My sister from another mother sharing the same Father; I love you dearly!

To Cedric Stykes, you were the pawn God used to get me here. HE had you plant the seed that would become me. You were never meant to be an existing factor in my life and for that revelation, I am now thankful…

All of my love,

Caneeka

Behind the Make-Up:

There are a few poems that I've written that are dear to my heart beyond just being a form of expression. Smeared Eyeliner and Faded Lipstick takes a look at the reality of every relationship and every form of love that I know people can relate to because I have talked to them. I have listened to their hearts and I have written on their behalf. This book is a compilation of love stories from all angles and because of those things I want to give a deeper look into those writings. Many of us, including myself, get in the habit of loving, hurting, and changing in secret. We parade around with foundation that doesn't match our skin and expect healing, happiness, and humility to appear.

It's up to US to encourage one another, motivate ourselves out of destruction, and remove our "makeup" in order to reveal our STRENGTH, our ACTIVISM, and our VISION. Where there is no vision the people perish. So let's wipe the metaphorical mascara from our eyes and begin to take hold of our destiny!

4 deeper meanings

On Breaks

Many years ago, when I was much younger, I met a guy who had it all. He had a promising career, very handsome, heavily involved in church, and could make women woo when they saw him walk. He had it going on! Or at least it appeared that way. As I grew to know him on a more personal level I learned he was very depressed, very troubled, and his self-esteem was non-existent. He was needy for something I couldn't give him and something he didn't know how to attain. His answer to his pain was to take his life. Suicide was a frequent choice for him despite me encouraging him otherwise. Helping to remind him of all he had to live for when someone is hurting none of those things matter. As I grew up, our relationship grew apart with moving and changes that occur in life. His story reminds me of how thick our makeup can get and if we fail to seek help the conclusion could be tragic.

I've heard of many suicides occur this year alone and I encourage you to watch for signs of those suffering in silence.

If you know someone who might be on the path of no return contact the National Suicide Prevention Lifeline at **1-800-273-TALK (8255)**, a free, 24-hour hotline available to anyone in suicidal crisis or emotional distress. Or visit http://www.suicidepreventionlifeline.org/

On Naïve

I witnessed my mother be a victim of domestic violence for a good duration of my early childhood. From that experience I have been a firm believer and fighter for ending violence against women through education. I wrote Naïve from the perspective I had of what domestic violence looks like. I think many people have a skewed perception of what the victim of domestic violence looks like and because it is such a taboo subject the majority of people have the, "see no evil, hear no evil, speak no evil" attitude towards the situation.

If I can open up one person's eyes about the subject, encourage one person to take a stand that they believe in to help educate women and men on increasing awareness then I will feel like I have done my part with working towards a goal greater than myself. For more information on how you can help end violence against women visit: http://www.now.org/issues/violence/ or you can check with your area for volunteer opportunities.

On February 13th

I have never met my father. I know that is the story for so many women growing up in today's society. He and I have talked on the phone, I've seen pictures of he and I when I was a baby but I do not have any memory of any type of interaction with him ever. In my experience with writing him and calling him it became a frustrating situation for me because he lives a few states over from me. Close enough to fly and feasible enough to drive.

So when I wrote February 13th I was thinking about all of those things plus the broken promises wrapped up in this holiday where you share your love with that special person in your life. Even though I was fortunate having great male influential figures in my life, a wonderful husband, and I completed and received my Bachelors Degree, the only thing I wanted that year for Valentines Day was my father. A phone call, a visit, or a card to let me know that he isn't just a figment of my imagination would have bridged the lack of connection we have had. Nonetheless I have learned that people are in your life and not in your life for good reason and the best thing to do is learn to embrace those people from afar for the impact they have made whether it has been good or bad.

Some interesting facts straight from the floor of the US Senate:
Source - Senate Concurrent Resolution 121

(1) In approximately 84 percent of the cases where a parent is absent, that parent is the father;

(2) If current trends continue, half of all children born today will live apart from one of their parents, usually their father, at some point before they turn 18 years old;

(4) Committed and responsible fathering during infancy and early childhood contributes to the development of emotional security, curiosity, and math and verbal skills;

(5) An estimated 19,400,000 children (27 percent) live apart from their biological fathers; and

(6) 40 percent of the children under age 18 not living with their biological fathers had not seen their fathers even once in the past 12 months, according to national survey data;

71% of high school dropouts come from fatherless homes. National Principals Association Report on the State of High Schools.

Fatherless boys and girls are: twice as likely to drop out of high school; twice as likely to end up in jail; four times more likely to need help for emotional or behavioral problems. US D.H.H.S. news release, March 26, 1999.

43% of US children live without their father. US Department of Census.

On Changing Pace

I've heard many stories about waiting for the right moment. For the right person to run over "me" with the flood gates of love. However, when those gates are opened, when that moment comes, when that person takes love/being in love to the next level that you've always dreamed of you RUN...

And once you get to your destination you realize how lonely you feel. How you think that perhaps you may have ruined the new chapter of your story and you think, "next time I will be ready. I'm just not ready right now."

But you are ready... you're just afraid.
Afraid to let someone love you more than you love yourself. Afraid to give in to feeling something other than pain and distress. But we don't admit to that! Oh no... We blame it on every element but fear and we end up wondering how we ended up in a place so empty...

Let's STOP running from quality people, STOP running from quality relationships, STOP running from being happy because we think we don't deserve it, STOP placing expectations on those who are doing the right thing, and STOP complaining about not being with someone when we destroy every opportunity we have for something worthwhile and let's START letting love embrace us like lilac lovers from head to toe!

On Dust Biting

Although I have been writing for a while, meeting, and talking to women about their relationships I have discovered just in the year of 2009 that there are many women willing to compromise who they are, how they deserve to be treated as women, and what they want in a relationship to be with someone they "think" they should be with. They have lacked the confidence to move forward to open up their options for someone better, more mature, and sure of who they are as men, so they end up repeating this cycle of complacency.

So many women and men fall in love with the potential a person has but they miss all of the signs that tell them this person doesn't care for you the way you love or care for them. That makes the situation unbalanced to begin with so why continue to bite the dust for a possibility. It's an epidemic and we need to help our friends, sisters, brothers, cousins, neighbors, mothers, aunts, uncles, fathers etc., learn that there is more to being in love, getting married, or dating than the "what could happen" if they let it. If they let you or if they let WE exist…

On White Lady

I love writing about things that are not as though they seem. The title, what it's for, and the figurative language throughout will evoke certain thoughts that I am writing about an addiction to a particular drug. Which is partially true but if you know my writing style and my creativity it will be easy to see that I am talking about my obsession with pen and paper. My need to write to the point that I can't think about anything else, I don't want to do anything else, and because of that desire, people that have other desires fail to understand mine.

Sometimes called the dream killers they want to be the ones to tell you that your dream and your hearts desire is a waste of time but if you can impact the world who are they to judge. The only people that I have met that understand this are other writers and with this kinship we challenge others to think outside of the box.

On The Surrogates (a poem)

Let's face it we all have a type… There are qualities we look for in a significant other that correlates with our preferences. Whether it's physical or intellectual or financial we all have something we like.

The Surrogates (a poem) is a true story and I wrote it more so out of shock than anything else. I think there should be a moment when we learn how to compromise on the physical for a relationship based on things with more substance. Sometimes as women we get so caught in the how a man looks we let him get away with anything because he's cute. We're hurting in the process but at least he's cute… right? We need to get back to the basics of loving ourselves first, not getting caught up in long eyelashes and "good hair" and learn to put our happiness first even if it means letting go. What good is being with someone that's cute if you lose yourself in the process…

Take a stand, learn to bend, but more importantly learn to walk away.

On Call her Me

At one point in life I was a teenager. Growing up in a place where body image was more important than anything else. The thought process that my body was more important that my brain or what I had to say out of my mouth was a battle I fought for years.

To see that same thought process still being carried out among young girls today is heart wrenching. Girls are immune to the words slut, hoe, and whore that they respond to those faster than their actual birth names. In my work with adolescents I've discovered that the positive reinforcement stops at the door. Parents have become too busy, to disconnected, and to oblivious to the importance of giving compliments and words of encouragement to their children that being labeled a hoe is something MORE than what they've ever received. So they embrace it because it's something to embrace and they work to live up to the label.

It tears me to pieces and if we fail to build up our youth, men and women, we will continue to watch babies, watch babies for the sake of having someone love them more than anyone else ever cared to share they did...

On The Big Bang

I got married in 2007 and I noticed things about marriage that people neglected to inform me about prior to the "I do's." Everyone that is married gives the same advice, which is, "The first year is the hardest. If you guys can make it "through" the first year you'll be okay." Everyone has their own philosophies and I noticed that "getting through" the first year wasn't going to be a problem for us because we didn't allow the enemy a stepping stone to create destruction in our marriage. However, I did notice that as love increases so does the weight. When I confronted family members and friends that had been married past the 10 year mark I asked them why they failed to leave out that extra love comes along with the vows and their response... laughter.

I wrote The Big Bang with the actual theory in mind of how some scholars describe the beginning of the earth's creation. Women are constantly bombarded with images of what we should or should not look like and that objectification found on magazine covers and billboards only encourage the decrease of self worth and appreciation. We forget how to value our bodies and who we are, what we have, and how to lift up our fellow women in their struggle against negative body image. I must admit I was concerned at first but of course for the wrong reasons. Many women or girls lack the knowledge of how to embrace growing breasts and getting a more voluptuous shape as it comes with age and apparently marriage, ;) and often times will find themselves using their bodies as a way to get attention.

The poem The Big Bang describes my "theory" on the different phases women will find themselves in as our bodies change over time and we lack the ability to embrace each entity.

We view change as something horrific when we should be focused on making sure we stay healthy and not necessarily model thin. Spiritually I believe that God created the earth and with that he created us in His image.

Ladies and Gentlemen, may we embrace our bodies, the changes it will encounter, and focus on leading healthy lives: the physical, the mental, and the spiritual.

<u>www.loveyourbody.nowfoundation.org</u>

On Metamorphosis

I found out I was expecting in October 2010. Even though I knew one day I would be the carrier of what would become my child I was in no way prepared for the shock my body was about to embark on. Moving into the second portion of this journey I am learning to embrace each change my body makes because I recognize that someone needs it more than I ever will understand.

It's scary, it's beautiful, it's hilarious, it's painful at times, it's an experience we're having together and discovering the new levels of love makes it all worth it!

2 Corinthians 3:18
"Our faces, then, are not covered. We all show the Lord's glory, and we are being changed to be like him. This change in us brings ever greater glory, which comes from the Lord, who is the Spirit" (NCV).

www.ingramcontent.com/pod-product-compliance
Lightning Source LLC
Chambersburg PA
CBHW060157050426
42446CB00013B/2862